COOL CLIVE

MICHAELA MORGAN

Illustrated by Dee Shulman

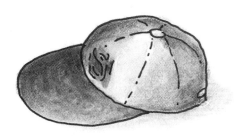

PACIFIC
LEARNING

05 04 03 02 01
10 9 8 7 6 5 4 3 2 1

Published by
Pacific Learning
P.O. Box 2723
Huntington Beach, CA 92647-0723
www.pacificlearning.com

ISBN: 1-59055-000-5
PL-7300

Contents

Chapter 1

These are the kids in my class.

They have the right haircuts.
They have the right clothes – the jeans,
the shirts, the caps, and the shoes.

I may not be the tallest kid.
I may not be the brightest kid either.
The one thing I do know is that I'm
really cool. The trouble is that my clothes
are just not cool at all.

"So what. I don't care," I say to myself
every morning – but I do care.

"You can wear my baseball hat today,"
my best friend says, but it's not the same.

My mom says,

My friend agrees with her. Actually, I know she's right too. It doesn't really matter. It *shouldn't* matter – but it does matter to me.

I want to look like my friends.

I want to look cool.

In my mind I can see exactly what I could look like.

I say,

So I say, "Can I have some shirts like those?"

Then Mom says, "You have plenty of your cousins' old shirts that you haven't even grown into yet."

When I say, "Look at those shoes, Mom. Do you think we could...?"

She says, "I'm sorry, Clive. We just can't afford them."

It seems like almost everything I have belonged to someone else before me.

Unfortunately, fashions have changed a little since my cousins were my age.

At school we all had to make up a rap about ourselves. This is mine:

I have the wrong shoes,
my haircut is lame,
my shirt has no labels,
have to pretend I look
the same.

So I set
the style with
my friends.
They're cool
and they know
the trends.
I have the
coolest of
super-cool
friends!

I don't feel better, though.

Chapter 2

I know exactly what I want. I've seen them in a sporting goods store.

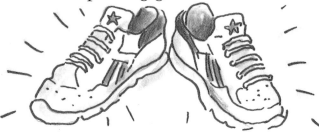

I also know exactly what my mom will say:

I dream about those stupid shoes.

Maybe I could find some long-lost treasure and buy them.

Maybe I could earn a reward and buy them.

Maybe I could get a job and…

That's what I'll do! I'll earn the money to buy those shoes.

It's not easy finding a job, especially when you're my age.

First I looked in the newspaper.

WANT ADS

WANT

For Hire:
Assistant Hairdresser.
No nose rings!
555-9843

Secretaries
Needed.
Will train
on phones.
555-3498

Psychic
No crystal balls.
555-9873

Plumber needed
fast. Bring tall
boots!

Gardeners
Bring own shovel. 555-9875

Experienced
Salespers
Apply no
555-43

Wanted:
Sales Clerk
Must be 16+.
34 Stone St.

Bus Drivers
If you have good driving
pply to join our team
fax: 555 6987

They were all jobs for grown-ups or older kids. There was nothing for me. What could I do?

I could look at the flyers hanging in the window of the corner store.

There were plenty of cards:

FOR SALE

Ping-pong table
1 paddle
No legs

555-7765

Three adorable
baby bunnies
for sale.
Only $10 each.

Call: 555-9213

Typewriter for sale

Perfect working order

555-9876

NEWSPAPER DELIVERY
BOYS AND GIRLS WANTED.

APPLY WITHIN

That's the one for me!

I'll get a job, save the money, and
I'll be Cool Clive, the Coolest Kid Alive.

When I asked the man at the counter
about the job, he said,

You're not big
enough, not old
enough, and not
strong enough.
Come back when
you're older.

Outside the store I met Rick Hamley, who is two years older than I am. He had a newspaper route. He was dragging his bag behind him, and he was looking hot and tired.

I need help. Tell your mom I'll keep an eye on you. You can start tomorrow at 6:30.

Six-thirty?
Six-thirty!
Surely he didn't mean six-thirty in the morning!!!
He did.

That night I was so excited I could hardly sleep. I'd asked my mom if I could help Rick with his paper route, and, after a while, she had agreed.

She helped me set the alarm clock for five-thirty, and she made me go to bed extra early.

It's hard to go to sleep when it's still light. All my plans were racing through my head. They started to sound like a song that went around and around and around…

I'll go and deliver the news, I'll earn cash to buy shoes.
They'll be cool and snazzy, bright and jazzy.
I'll go to school, looking so great, looking so cool.

Friends will say "Hey, look at Clive! He's the coolest kid alive."

In the end I fell asleep, and then...

It was time to get up and get started on my first day of delivering the papers with Rick.

MONDAY was very wet.	TUESDAY was no better.

WEDNESDAY was worse.	THURSDAY was even wetter.

Still, I kept going...

FRIDAY...	SATURDAY....

On Sunday, the newspapers were very thick and heavy.

I heaved that bag.	I hauled that bag.

I nearly gave up, but I kept going and I got paid. YIPPEE!

The next day I met Rick.

22

23

Chapter 3

I went home and counted my money.

I wrote down what I had and what I needed. Then I took a break.

I was worn out and fed up and I still needed tons more money.

The next day I went back to the store. I didn't go in, in case there were any more unhappy customers in there, but I read the ads that were hanging outside.

There were a few new ones.

FOR SALE

Set of
dining room chairs
by family with solid
wooden bottoms.

555-7765

Ten adorable
baby bunnies
for quick sale.
Only $7 each.

Call: 555-92B

Dog Walker wanted

Take my dog on one long
walk a day and earn extra
spending money.

34 Park Walk, Oaktown

YES! That's the job for me!

I wrote down the address, asked my
mom, and walked over to learn more
about the job.

"You're not very old," the lady said. "You're not very big... but you are the only one who was interested in the job. I'll give you a try."

She handed me a leash and out bounced...

Toodles!

"Now just take Toodles around the park once, then bring him right back home. Don't let him get tired. Don't let him get dirty. Remember, once around the park and then bring little Toodles right back home."

She told me what to do over and over
and over again. I wish she'd told the dog.
Toodles had a mind of his own.
We went around the park once.
No problem.

Then Toodles decided to go around the
park again...

No, Toodles!

and again...

and again.

We visited the ducks. Toodles liked the water.

We visited the flower beds. Toodles liked the mud and the fertilizer.

We visited the trash cans. Toodles liked the garbage.

Then Toodles decided to go home – the short way.

His owner was not pleased... not pleased at all.

She paid me for one day but said,

I went home, counted my money,
wrote the amount in my book, then took
a nap.

From time to time I went back to the store. Sometimes there were new ads:

FOR SALE

Baby crib from family with a screw loose.

555-7765

25 Rabbits FREE to good home

Call: 555-92B anytime!

Duck and chicks Cheap! 555-9831

There was only one job:

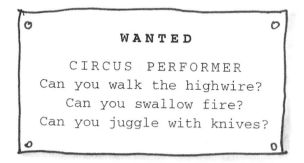

WANTED

CIRCUS PERFORMER
Can you walk the highwire?
Can you swallow fire?
Can you juggle with knives?

That was NOT the job for me.

That was when I decided to start my own business.

I made posters:

and leaflets:

Your car was flashy
but now it's splashy
what do you do?

CALL CLIVE

CLIVE'S CAR
CLEANING
AND ODD JOBS
555-4321

I borrowed a bucket,

a sponge,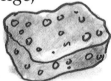

 and a towel.

Off I went.

I was doing very well, amazingly well actually, when...

I was pretty lucky. I didn't damage the car. I didn't fall in the pond, but...

I did break a few things.

I said, "I'm very sorry.
It was an accident.
I'll pay for the damage."

And I did.

Now all I had left was my soggy
sponge, my towel, and my bucket with
a hole in it.

Can you imagine how I felt?

I was trudging home by the park when I heard:

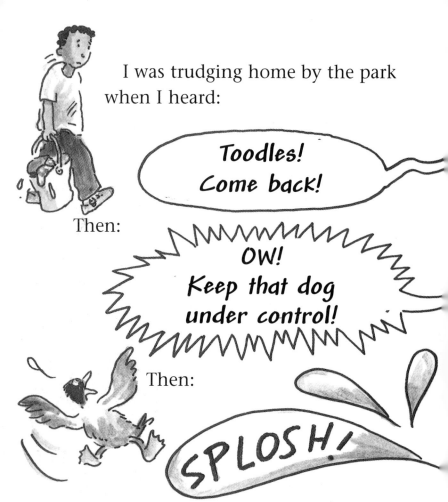

**Toodles!
Come back!**

Then:

**OW!
Keep that dog under control!**

Then:

SPLOSH!

A crowd of people were gathered by the duck pond. I went to take a look and got there just in time to see a man crawling out of the water. He was wet and covered in pond slime. He didn't look happy at all.

Gaz and Rick were trying to pull
Toodles away and apologize to the
man at the same time.

Chapter 4

Floating in the middle of the pond was his briefcase. It was slowly bobbing around and drifting in circles.

"It's full of very important papers," the man said. "Oh no! It's going to sink! Get a fishing net quick!" he yelled.

No such luck. The briefcase was sinking and no one had a fishing net.

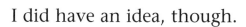

I did have an idea, though.

I used my towel, my bucket with a hole in, and a long stick, and…

39

"Thank you. Thank you. THANK YOU!" said the man. "You saved all my papers and money. I would like to reward you."

He reached into his soggy bag and...	I held my breath and wished.

Money? Money to buy my shoes?

Then he pulled out...	a soggy little card

	with an address on it.

"Stop by and see me," he said.
Then he left, leaving nothing
behind but a patch of damp grass and
some pond slime.

I went home and told my mom all about it.

So I had to wait until Saturday, which was the next day she had off work.

In a way I was glad she was there. It was a weird place. It was a big warehouse in a side street, all huge and dusty and full of boxes.

It was kind of spooky.

I turned to
my mom,
but she wasn't
listening.
She was staring at a
huge pile of boxes.

44

The man was busy telling me all about his job. "I bring in all these things from the factories where they're made, and I sell them to local stores."

"I've seen some of these in store windows," I said.

"Why don't you help yourself to a few of these things," the man said.

"Oh, we couldn't," my mom said.

"Yes, you could," the man agreed. "Your son saved me a lot of money and a lot of trouble. I want to reward him!"

So I got a baseball cap, and some jeans, a T-shirt, and the shoes.

Cool!

In my new shirt I felt brighter. In my new shoes I felt taller. I looked the way I'd always known I could –

Cool Clive, the coolest kid alive!

About the Author

I write all sorts of stories, and I also like to write poems, so I particularly enjoyed writing *Cool Clive*, a story that has rhymes and raps in it.

I often visit schools, and I got the idea for this story when I was talking to a group of children. I noticed that they were all wearing the latest brand-name clothes – all except one. I decided to write that boy's story.

Michaela Morgan